GARBAGE TRUCKS
at Work

D. R. Addison

PowerKiDS press.

New York

For my little truck experts, Deming, Riley, and Hannah

Published in 2009 by The Rosen Publishing Group, Inc.
29 East 21st Street, New York, NY 10010

First Edition

Editor: Joanne Randolph
Book Design: Greg Tucker
Photo Researcher: Jessica Gerweck

Photo Credits: Cover, pp. 17, 21 Shutterstock.com; p. 5 © istockphoto.com/Niilo Tippler; p. 7 © istockphoto.com; p. 9 © istockphoto.com/Mike Clarke; p. 11 © istockphoto.com/Gina Addison; p. 13 © istockphoto.com/Brian Daly; p. 15 © Getty Images; p. 19 © istockphoto.com/Sava Miokovic; p. 23 © Natalie Kauffman/Getty Images.

Library of Congress Cataloging-in-Publication Data

Addison, D. R.
  Garbage trucks at work / D. R. Addison. — 1st ed.
      p. cm. — (Big trucks)
  Includes index.
  ISBN 978-1-4358-2699-1 (library binding) — ISBN 978-1-4358-3085-1 (pbk.)
ISBN 978-1-4358-3091-2 (6-pack)
  1. Refuse collection vehicles—Juvenile literature. 2. Refuse and refuse disposal—Juvenile literature.
I. Title.
  TD794.A424 2009
  628.4'42—dc22
                                    2008021612

Manufactured in the United States of America

Contents

This is a **garbage** truck. It has a big job.

87

5

The garbage truck picks up **trash**. It keeps our streets clean.

The garbage goes in the back of the truck.

The garbage truck has a part that presses on the trash to make it smaller.

Now there is room for more garbage. The driver heads to the next stop.

Sometimes **garbage collectors** ride holding on to the back of the truck.

When the truck stops, the workers jump off. They dump trash from the garbage cans into the back.

Some garbage trucks pick up all the glass, cans, and paper we have used.

Dump, dump, dump goes the garbage truck. All the trash is in the **landfill** now.

Good job, garbage truck! Thanks for keeping our streets so clean.

Words to Know

garbage

garbage collector

landfill

trash

Index

Web Sites

Due to the changing nature of Internet links, PowerKids Press has developed an online list of Web sites related to the subject of this book. This site is updated regularly. Please use this link to access the list:

www.powerkidslinks.com/bigt/garbage/

24